Dear Grandma,

Your story is very valuable to me and I would like to preciously keep it to pass it on.

In this book you will find questions about your life that you may or may not answer. Write what you want to write, it is your story.

If you want, you can add photos or even a recipe!

Take as much time as you need to complete this book. When you finish, you can return it to me.

....

....

....

....

....

....

Special Request

Dear Customers,

Thank you for your trust.

I publish my books independently.

If you like this journal, please feel to leave me

a comment on Amazon. I read each your comments

carefully: they are crucial to support my work and

allow me to offer you new quality content.

I hope you enjoy this journal as much as

I enjoyed designing it!

Scan this QR code
to leave your comment:

In advance, a big thank you!
Lise

USA　　　　**UK**　　　　**CA**　　　　**AUS**

Table of contents

Your family tree

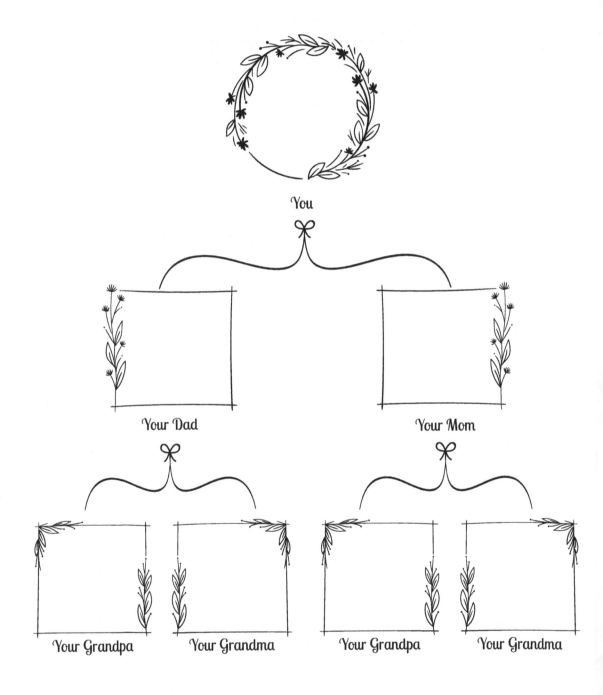

You

Your Dad

Your Mom

Your Grandpa

Your Grandma

Your Grandpa

Your Grandma

Let's talk about you, Grandma

Paste a picture of you

Your name is ....

You were born on .... in ....

You have .... child(ren) .... grandchild(ren) and ....

great-grandchild(ren).

Your childhood

Tell me about your parents: where did they come from, how did they meet, what did they do for a living, what were they like?

Your Mom:

....

....

....

....

....

....

....

....

....

....

....

....

....

....

....

....

....

Your Dad:

....

....

....

....

....

....

....

....

....

....

....

....

....

....

....

....

....

....

....

....

What are your fondest memories with them?

....

....

....

....

....

....

....

....

....

....

....

....

Tell me about your brothers and sisters.

....

....

....

Did you get along well with them? What did you play?

....

....

....

....

....

....

....

Did you know your grandparents? What were they like?

....
....
....
....
....
....
....
....
....
....
....

Did they live nearby?

....
....
....
....
....

Did they babysit you?

....
....
....
....
....
....

Family memories (photos or anecdotes)

Where did you live?

....
....
....
....

What was your house like?

....
....
....
....
....
....
....
....
....
....
....

What about your room?

....
....
....
....
....
....
....

Were you a well-behaved or rambunctious child?

....
....
....
....
....

How often were you scolded at home? What were your punishments?

....
....
....
....
....

What toys did you have? Did you have a blanket?

....
....
....
....
....
....
....
....
....

What was your school like?

....
....
....
....
....

How did you get there? (by foot, by bike...)

....
....
....
....
....

Do you remember your teachers? Was there one who left a particular impression?

....
....
....
....
....
....
....
....
....
....
....

Did you work well or did you have difficulties?

....

....

....

....

....

....

What was your favorite subject?

....

....

Did you have many friends? What was your best friend's name?
Do you still see her?

....

....

....

....

....

....

....

....

....

....

What did you play in the playground?

....
....
....
....
....
....
....
....

What were the punishments at school?

....
....
....
....
....
....
....
....

When you were little, what career did you dream of?

....
....
....
....
....

Outside of school, did you do any activities or sports?

....
....
....
....
....

Did you cook with your mom? If so, do you remember a family recipe (you have room on the next page to write it down)?

....
....
....
....
....

Did you have a party every year for your birthday? Do you remember one in particular?

....
....
....
....
....
....
....
....
....

Family recipe

What did you do at Christmas? Was there one that particularly stood out to you?

....
....
....
....
....
....
....
....
....
....
....
....
....
....
....

What was the best gift you ever received? What was the occasion?

....
....
....
....
....
....
....
....

Did you go on vacation? If so, what is your fondest memory?

....

....

....

....

....

....

....

....

....

....

....

What did you do during summer vacations?

....

....

....

....

....

....

....

....

....

Family memories (photos or anecdotes)

Your adolescence

What was your adolescence like?

....
....
....
....
....
....
....
....
....
....

What kind of music did you listen to?

....
....
....
....
....
....
....
....

How was the fashion? How did you dress?

....

....

....

....

....

....

....

....

What did you like to do in your free time?

....

....

....

....

....

....

....

Did you go to the movies? To the theater? To concerts?

....

....

....

....

....

What did you study?

....

....

....

....

....

....

....

....

Did you choose them or were they imposed on you?

....

....

....

....

....

....

....

....

....

Memories of your adolescence (photos or anecdotes)

Your adult life

When did you start working?

....

....

What did you do?

....

....

....

....

....

....

How did you get to work? How far away was it?

....

....

....

....

Were you still living with your parents?

....

....

....

At what age did you meet Grandpa?

....
....
....
....

How did you meet him?

....
....
....
....
....
....
....
....
....
....
....
....
....
....
....
....
....
....

Was he your first love?

....
....
....
....
....
....
....
....

What did you like about him?

....
....
....
....
....
....
....
....
....
....
....
....
....
....
....

How did he propose?

....
....
....
....
....
....
....
....
....
....

And how did your entourage react?

....
....
....
....
....
....
....
....
....
....
....
....

Tell me about your wedding!

Photos of your wedding

Did you go on your honeymoon?

....

....

....

....

....

....

....

....

....

....

When did you move in together? What was your first home like?

....

....

....

....

....

....

....

....

....

....

....

....

Did you have hobbies? Did you travel ?

....
....
....
....
....
....
....
....
....
....

What is your fondest memory of that time with Grandpa?

....
....
....
....
....
....
....
....
....

Your life as a Mom

At what age did you become a mother for the first time?

....
....

How did you react when you found out you were pregnant?

....
....
....
....
....

What changed the most in your life the day you became a mom?

....
....
....
....
....
....
....
....
....
....

Did you raise your child/children differently than your parents raised you?

....
....
....
....
....
....
....
....
....
....

What are you most proud of in your life as a mom?

....
....
....
....
....
....
....
....
....
....
....
....

How was the birth of my mom/dad? Was Grandpa present at the birth?

....
....
....
....
....
....
....
....
....
....

What were the first years like? Were you working or staying home taking care of mom/dad?

....
....
....
....
....
....
....
....
....

Which baby was she/he? Did she/he cry a lot?

....
....
....
....
....
....

Do you remember a song you sang to her/him or a story you told her/him?

....
....
....
....
....
....
....

What was his/her favorite food?

....
....
....
....
....
....
....
....

Do you remember her/his first day of school? Was it hard?

....

....

....

....

....

....

....

....

....

....

Did you go on a family vacation? Do you remember any particular vacation?

....

....

....

....

....

....

....

....

....

....

....

....

....

Memories with Mom / Dad (photos or anecdote)

What was my mom / dad like as a teenager?

....
....
....
....
....
....
....
....
....
....

When did she / he first introduce you to my mom / dad?
How did you and Grandpa react?

....
....
....
....
....
....
....
....
....
....

Your life as a Grandmother

At what age did you become a grandmother for the first time?

....

....

How did it feel?

....

....

....

....

....

....

....

....

Do you do the same activities with me as with Mom / Dad?

....

....

....

....

....

....

....

....

What do you like best when you are with me?

....

....

....

....

....

....

....

....

....

Are there any things you didn't allow Mom / Dad to do but you let me do?

....

....

....

....

....

....

....

....

....

....

....

What are your fondest memories with me?

....
....
....
....
....
....
....
....
....
....

Are there still things you would like to do with me?

....
....
....
....
....
....
....
....
....
....
....

How big do you love me?

Memories with Me (photos or anecdotes)

Your whole life

What are the best moments of your life so far?

....

....

....

....

....

....

....

....

....

....

....

....

....

....

....

....

....

....

....

The most beautiful people you have met?

The most beautiful places you have visited?

The most beautiful things you have seen?

Have you had any difficult moments that you would like to tell me about?

What lessons have you learned from them?

What are your dreams?

Is there anything you haven't done yet that you would really like to do in your life?

What memories would you like to be remembered for?

What advice would you give me to succeed in my personal life?

And for my professional life?

I also wanted to tell you...

A little room for what you want to add…

....
....
....
....
....
....
....
....
....
....
....
....
....
....
....
....
....
....
....

Your life in pictures

Made in the USA
Monee, IL
13 December 2022

21351163R00044